MW01533799

The Book on God's Healing Code

Is Removing Painful Emotions Safe for Christians? Is Energy Healing Safe?

Doris Morissette

Copyright © 2022 by Doris Morissette

All rights reserved. No part of this publication may be reproduced, stored, or transmitted in any form or by any means, electronic, mechanical, photocopying, recording, scanning, or otherwise, without written permission from the publisher. It is illegal to copy this book, post it to a website, or distribute it by any other means without permission.

Doris Morissette asserts the moral right to be identified as the author of this work.

Doris Morissette has no responsibility for the persistence or accuracy of URLs for external or third-party Internet websites referred to in this publication and does not guarantee that any content on such websites is, or will remain, accurate or appropriate.

Information in this book is not intended to replace the advice of the reader's own physician or other medical professionals. You should consult a medical professional in matters relating to health, especially if you have existing medical conditions, and before starting, stopping, or changing the dose of any medications you are taking, or implementing a new health routine. Individual readers are solely responsible for their own healthcare decisions. The author and the publisher do not accept responsibility for any adverse effects individuals may claim to experience, whether directly or indirectly, from the information contained in this book.

Not everyone will find immediate relief from their ailments by applying energy healing methods. However, since 2017, my experience applying energy healing modalities, I, as well as other practitioners/coach, have seen some amazing results. Many people have used these energy healing principles to support physical and emotional freedom from problems they have struggled with for years.

Scripture quotations marked "TPT" are from The Passionate Translation®. Copyright © 2017, 2018, 2020 by Passion & Fire Ministries, Inc. Used by permission. All rights reserved. thepassiontranslation.com

Scripture quotations marked "NIV" are from THE HOLY BIBLE, NEW INTERNATIONAL VERSION, NIV® Copyright © 1973, 1978, 1984, 2011 by Biblica, Inc.® Used by permission. All rights are reserved worldwide.

Scripture quotations marked "TLB" are taken from *The Living Bible*, copyright © 1971 by Tyndale House Foundation. Used by permission of the Tyndale House Publishers, Carol Stream, Illinois 60188. All rights reserved.

Scripture quotations marked "AMPC" are taken from The Holy Bible: The Amplified Bible. 1987. 2015. La Habra, CA: The Lockman Foundation. As found in the Logos Bible study software program and the e-Sword.

This book is dedicated to truth-seekers who want to receive all that God has created.

"Never doubt God's mighty power to work in you and accomplish all this. He will achieve infinitely more than your greatest request, your most unbelievable dream, and exceed your wildest imagination!" Ephesians 3:20-21 TPT.

Contents

What People Are Saying About Doris Morissette

J esus told us to judge a tree by its fruit. My gratitude goes to these clients who wanted to share their stories with you. What you will read below is the result of God's hand working through our sessions. Be prepared to suspend your unbelief.

Client #1, Liz from Florida:

Liz from Florida has a captivating story about a radical change in her relationship with the Lord, amongst other benefits received. Her story is found in Chapter 8.

Client #2, Krista from Wyoming

Krista needed two recreative miracles, and she got them! I have to make this clear now. These miracles did not happen because of The Emotion Code. Not directly. It was during the session that she commented to me that her feet were cold. After she told me about her situation, the word of the Lord came to me that she had the faith to receive two recreative miracles at that moment. We paused the session and began to pray. Our prayers were answered on the spot. Her story is also in Chapter 8.

Client #3, Sua from Ontario, Canada:

"I am so grateful to God that He led me to Doris. For over a decade, I lived in an unhealthy relationship where my ex-husband's daily criticism, judgment, and explosive anger behaviors rendered me powerless. Although I have removed myself from the relationship whenever my ex-husband was in my place to help with the children, his attitude of anger still very much affected me. I would easily react to that old foe of anger like a magnet pulling me into negative emotions. I would feel so frustrated and blamed myself for not having the guts to tell him to leave."

"After 3 sessions with Doris, I noticed I was calmer and had more control of strong negative emotions when responding to the same old negative behaviors. For example, this past week my ex- and I had to work together on some family matters. On a couple of occasions, I watched him being so angry, but to my amazement; I didn't react or get pulled into the negative behavior like I normally had been. Instead, calmly, I observed the behavior pass by, and then I could speak firmly about the situation with no potent emotions. It felt powerful to be in control of my emotions and choose my words rather than reacting. Praise God for Doris. Thank you, Doris!"

Client #4, Nicole from New Jersey, USA:

"I am giving a review for Doris, which I rarely do, but because of Doris's ability and thoroughness in dealing with an issue and really getting in there, I am giving her a review of none other. She is truly born to be a healer; her long-standing career shows it as a nurse, and it shows in the work she has done with me. She can truly tackle any issue and she gets it from all different angles. Wow! It is truly amazing how she gets in there. Unbelievable results."

Client #5, Joan from Washington State, USA:

"Doris has such a soothing voice and presence that it nurtured me, along with her gentle unfolding of the possibilities of my car-sick dog."

These are just a few testimonies of many.

Introduction

The answers you have been searching for may have never been available to you. Now they are!

Explanations about Energy Healing may be simpler than you imagined; they don't have to be complicated.

Six years of research and experience have resulted in this book. We serve a loving Creator who left clues for us to figure things out. There is an appointed time for revelation. Now is the time.

This is how one of my clients responded after previewing this book:

> The energy concept feels safe to me now that I realize energy exists as an objective reality and is not just a "mystical" concept. Nicole Williamson, MBA (Master of Business Administration)

This is the first book in a series dedicated to help you **discover** your Godly inheritance.

You will find scriptural and scientific proof in the following chapters to help you decide if the Emotion Code, Body Code, and Energy Healing can be tools that God you can use in your life. Be prepared to suspend your unbelief! See you in Chapter 1.

1

Discover God's Healing Code

D id God give you a gift that you never opened? Join me now as we take a peek at some of His gifts.

The first gift is that God created humans in His image; to live forever. When he created Adam and Eve, He gave them the gift of free will to choose, and we all know the consequences of their choice.

This did not catch God by surprise. He had a remedy. Not only did his remedy include covering their shame, but He also provided a way to restore through the gift of the blood of Jesus what sin had allowed.[1] Genesis 3:15 and Colossians 1:19-20.

God is faithful and true. He provided for healing in the Old Testament and in the New.

Is God willing to heal us *now*?

Yes.[2] We read in Exodus, "I am the Lord, who heals you." 15:26 NIV.[3]Healing is another gift.

We are familiar with popular and acceptable assists with healing. Examples of these are the medical system, talk therapy, physiotherapy, and chiropractors. They are all established.

Sometimes the body needs help to heal itself and those systems are not helping.

God provided here as well. It lies on the periphery of acceptable healing assists. Its name? Energy Healing. Energy Healing is the topic of this book. Energy Healing is a gift, as well.

Just as God created the laws of gravity to keep our feet planted on the earth, he also created other laws which we discover in various branches of science. God is the creator of science. The truth we find in science points to God.

One of those branches of science we call physics is called "quantum". Quantum means energy. God is the source of all energy, and Energy Healing is rooted in this objective science.

God also writes in code; therefore, our universe contains code. One example of that is the genetic code.[4]

The genetic code is only one of the many codes God provided us with.

God is a God of life and the living. He infused life into all that He created. All that He created includes all the sciences. He put the answers and provisions in a coded form through all the various laws we find in operation throughout the universe.

It is up to us to find and use the gift of healing He provided. He wants us well. Shall we explore this gift? The question also is, do you have eyes to see this gift?

---

1. David C. Grabbe What The Bible Says About The Knowledge Of Good And Evil. Bible Tools. Retrieved 28 April 2022, from https://www.bibletools.org

2. The Body Can Heal Itself. Dr. William Li. Retrieved 28 April 2022, from https://drwilliamli.com/the-body-can-heal-itself/

3. Exodus 15:26 New International Version (NIV). (n.d.). Biblegateway.Com. Retrieved 28 April 2022, from https://www.biblegateway.com

4. Has Science Discovered God? (n.d.). Y-Jesus. Retrieved April 23, 2022, from https://y-jesus.com

2

Truth and Eyes to See

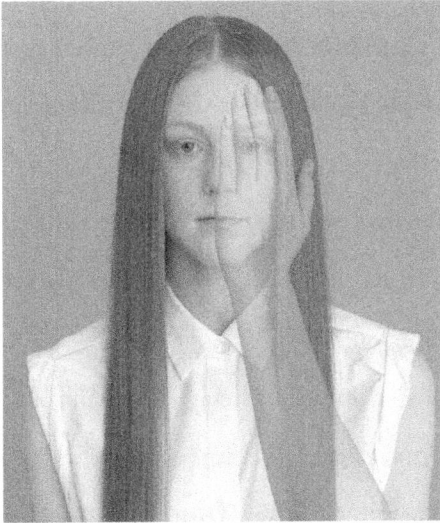

S cripture tells us that "the truth will set us free". John 8:36. Therefore, truth brings freedom, and His freedom is lasting.

Shall we explore the truth from God's word?

We read: "He came to the people he created-to those who should have received Him, but they did not recognize him." John 1:11 TPT.

Do we want to be like that? We want eyes to see and recognize!

How can we recognize unless we can see?

Here is just one example from science about perception being changed by seeing.

Mr. Hubble and his telescope showed the Milky Way was just a speck in the universe. Until then, scientists believed the Milky Way was the **only** galaxy in the universe.[1]

On the website Lumen Learning, we read: "When Hubble's paper on the distances to nebulae was read before a meeting of the American Astronomical Society on the first day of 1925, the entire room erupted in a standing ovation."[2]

Perceptions changed because of the invention and discovery of one person's work. The result? The scientists could now see the truth. It's wonderful when we can see.

We now have two examples of seeing. One example is from scripture regarding people not seeing. The other example is from science not seeing the truth regarding the Milky Way. What else are we not seeing?

Perhaps we are not seeing the fullness of the truth regarding Energy Healing either?

Let me explain what I mean by that.

Cell phones, and cars, for example, are tools. Right? Tools are something you use to accomplish a purpose.

Energy Healing is also a tool to accomplish a purpose.

Before you bought your cell phone or your car, did you research who created or invented it? Or did you investigate their religion? No?

Maybe the inventor was a Satanist or sorcerer, or someone not Christian? Have you ever considered that? No?

Does it even matter? Like cars and cell phones, Energy Healing is just a tool!

Yet, the inventor of one Energy Healing modality; called the Emotion Code, is often judged because of his religion. Dr. Bradley Nelson's Mormon religion may not align with some folks.

What we are doing here is judging tools by different standards. Double standards, in fact.

We judge one set of tools according to the religion of the discoverer of that tool, while we judge other sets of tools by their ability to be useful. That is what I meant by double standards.

Would it help if I told you that, unlike the car which operates according to Newtonian physics principles; Energy Healing operates according to quantum physics principles? Yet, both branches of science are but tools themselves.

OK, let's switch our vantage point from tools and seeing to intention now.

What was the intention of the inventors of your cell phone or your car? Who knows? Money?

What was the intention of Dr. Bradley Nelson regarding the tool of Emotion Code (a form of Energy Healing)?

His intention was to help his patients beyond what his training as a chiropractor could do. In his desperation for help, he asked God for help. In fact, he asked God the Father in the name of Jesus for wisdom.

I wonder if God the Father smiled at that request and thought, "finally someone is asking me for wisdom"?

Does that remind you of the Bible? It should! We read in the Bible: "And if anyone longs to be wise, ask God for wisdom and he will give it!" James 1:5 TPT.

Dr. Bradley Nelson followed the biblical principle of asking God for wisdom, and God provided wisdom according to his word.

If you are going to judge at all, please judge Dr. Bradley Nelson and his discovery of the Emotion Code by his intention. His intention was for wisdom. Please do not let the label of his religion prevent you from considering The Emotion Code as a healing modality.

Now, shall we return to the subject of "having eyes to see"?

Remember how the scientific discovery brought about by the Hubble telescope changed the perception of the size of the galaxy? Maybe our own perception can change as we also open our own eyes to see more truth revealed?

Are you interested in seeing more truth revealed? More truth awaits you in the next chapters.

---

1. Brian Resnick. (2016, December 30). How Edwin Hubble discovered galaxies outside our own. Vox. Retrieved May 1, 2022, from

https://www.vox.com/2016/11/20/13677046/edwin-hubble-and romeda-galaxy

2. The Discovery of Galaxies. (n.d.). Lumen Learning. Retrieved May 1, 2022, from

https://courses.lumenlearning.com/astronomy/chapter/the-disco very-of-galaxies/

3

Who Created Energy Healing?

T he picture is a picture of a potter working with clay at the potter's wheel. We see the potter molding clay. We read in Isiah 64:8 how God is our potter and we are his clay. God is our creator, as well as the creator of all there is.

We read in Genesis how in the beginning, God spoke everything into existence. The Bible does not use words like "physics", "law of gravity", "mathematical equations", "biofield", or "quantum physics", yet all these things have been awaiting our discovery.

God included everything in the beginning, even Energy Healing. Why do I mention this? Scripture tells us: "For in Him was created the universe of things, both in the heavenly realm and on the earth, all that is seen and all that is unseen." Colossians 1:16 TPT. It is Jesus, through whom and for whom all things were created, and it is Jesus who holds all things together.

"For nothing has its existence apart from Him." John 1:3 TPT.

Energy Healing is "unseen". However, "unseen" does not mean not present.

Energy is everywhere, as is Jesus, and we don't see either of them.

In this chapter, we learned that God created Energy Healing. So then, who was the first (Christian) energy healer?

4

Who Was the First Christian Energy Healer?

Jesus was the first energy healer as recorded in the Bible. He healed the woman with "the issue of blood."

In Mark chapter 5, we read about how this woman had been bleeding for twelve years. She heard Jesus was coming to town. She hoped he could help her. We read that not only did she spend all her money on doctors, but she continued to suffer, and her problem only grew worse. She knew her bleeding made her "unclean" and that anyone she touched would become unclean as well. Being unclean was a serious problem.

She thought, "If I just touch his clothes, I will be healed." (And so she touched his clothes.) Her bleeding stopped, and she felt in her body she became free from her suffering. Mark 5: 28-29 TPT.

Another story of healing involves the centurion and his servant. His servant was sick. The centurion understood authority. He said: "Lord, don't trouble yourself, for I do not deserve to have you come under my roof. That is why I did not even consider myself worthy to come to you. But say the word, and my servant will be healed. For I, myself, am a man under authority, with soldiers under me. I tell this one, 'Go,' and he goes; and that one, 'Come,' and he comes. I say to my servant, 'Do this,' and he does it." Luke 7:1-10 NIV.

Remember Jesus' answer? Jesus marveled at the centurion's faith. He said there was no greater faith in the whole of Israel. The subsequent healing of the centurion's servant was the first demonstration of "Energy Healing" done from a **distance**.

The Bible contains many stories of Jesus' healing.

Were we told to follow Jesus' example? And do "greater things"? How many people have done "greater things"? Isn't it about time we do "greater things"?

After all, we were told to "let our light shine" before others; so that they will give their praise to our Father in heaven. Matthew 5:16 TPT.

The light of Christ is within us if we are Christians. The bible also says that if we join to the vine (Jesus) we will bear much good fruit.

"I am the sprouting vine and you're my branches. As you live in union with me as your source, fruitfulness will stream from within you—but when you live separated from me, you are powerless." John 15:5 TPT.

Therefore, as Jesus bore fruit for the glory of God, so are we to follow his example. We can use the gift of Energy Healing to bring glory to God.

Ah, but you say, one code God created is the genetic code. Did God provide a way that can help change an ailing genetic code? Find out in the next chapter.

5

Can DNA Be Changed? Revealing the Secret Power of Words, Thoughts, and Frequencies.

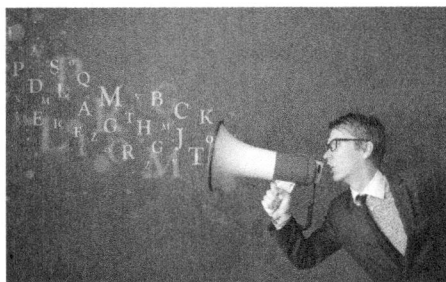

Y es! A resounding yes!

But first, let me reiterate the question from the previous chapter. The question was: "Did God provide a way that can help change an ailing genetic code?" I will answer this.

Next, we have to figure out what DNA has to do with the genetic code. We read on the genome.gov website: "Genetic code refers to the instructions within a gene to tell a cell how to make a specific protein. Each gene's code uses the four nucleotide bases of DNA..."[1]

So it seems to mean DNA is a part of the genetic code. So it is plausible that if you can affect the DNA, you could then affect the genetic code?

Therefore, our focus is now on the DNA itself.

We will see how DNA can be changed through words, thoughts, and even frequencies!

DNA is part of God's creation. DNA is alive.

We serve a God who is living. All that He created is alive. We read in scripture that the rocks and hills can "sing" (Isiah 55:12), that the trees can "clap their hands" (Isiah 55:12); that the rocks can "cry out" (Luke 19:40). We read in Job 38.7 about how the morning stars "sang" together. The words "sing", "clap their hands", "cry out", and "sang" all describe actions that a living person can do; therefore, we have to assume we are being told that nature is alive.

There are many more scriptures that show God's creation is alive. God's creation can also respond and communicate. To be brief, I have chosen not to provide the scientific examples of the fact that stars emit sound and how living vegetation also communicates. Science is proving the bible to be correct.

Would God's creation not reflect who he is? Would his creation not also respond to thought and intention? DNA is his creation as well.

The Bible shows how thought and intention can create change. We read: "Your ancestors have been taught, 'Never commit adultery.' However, I say to you, if you look with lust in your eyes at a woman who is not your wife, you've already committed adultery in your heart." Matthew 5:27-28 TPT.

That is a clear biblical correlation of our creative role regarding intention and thought. Our thoughts and intention play an integral role in creation. The Bible verse shows how thought can be a valid part of creation.

The act of speaking is the next step after intention.

God began our cosmos as we know it by speaking it into being. As God spoke all into existence, so we can follow his example. This brings him glory.

Science is catching up to the bible. Next, three specific scientific examples show how the power of voice, thoughts, and frequencies can change the structure of DNA. After all, DNA is alive and responsive.

Are you ready?

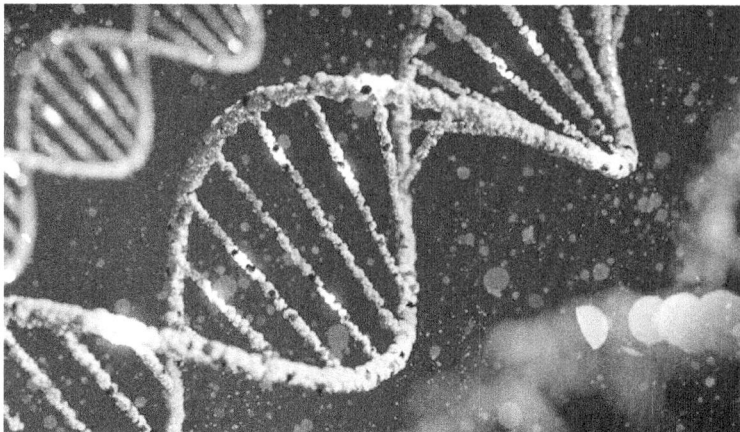

The first source comes from Dr. Joe Dispenza's book "Breaking the Habit of Being Yourself"[2] which shows that our thoughts affect our DNA.

He writes about how the Heart Math Institute carried out an experiment regarding how DNA could be affected from a distance. They had three groups attempting to effect a change in the DNA. Only one group could affect the DNA. This group used thought (intention) and emotion only. It was possible to unwind the DNA by 25%.

The second source comes from a book written in German called "Vernetzte Intelligenz"[3] by von Grazyna Fosar and Franz Bludorf. In that book, the authors detailed the investigations by Russian researchers into the 90% of the DNA labeled as "junk". They concluded that part of the purpose of our DNA is for communication and data storage; that DNA functions as an antenna that can transmit and receive communication.

The Russian biophysicist and molecular biologist Pjotr Garjajev[4] and his colleagues found DNA reacts to voice, radio waves, and frequencies. That means that we may be able to change our DNA. Here is the reason: "Living chromosomes function just like solitonic-holographic computers using the endogenous DNA laser radiation."

According to the authors of that book, DNA is a transmitter and receiver.

God provided us with receivers and transmitters as part of our DNA. This is another clue showing "Energy Healing" derives from God.

Science discovered what God put there already.

I am trying to remain brief in my statements to present this idea to you. It is intentional on my part to not give you exhaustive explanations of the book written by Grazyna Fosar and Franz Bludorf. I have done this to keep things simple.

The third source is recorded in a journal called Advances[5] in 1993 and is referred to in an article called Quantum Biology.[6]

The results of the following experiment have now become famous. This was an experiment conducted by Army scientists. These scientists got a sample of DNA from a subject which they then placed in a distant room hundreds of feet away, under careful monitoring. The scientists wanted to see if the DNA would respond to the emotions of the person sampled. It did!

The DNA showed powerful electrical responses as recorded by precise instruments at the same moment as the person experiencing those emotions.

Scientists repeated the experiment. This time, the scientists placed the DNA 350 miles away from the person. The results were identical to the earlier experiment. Distance did not affect the response of DNA. The scientists concluded that distance has no effect on the emotion and DNA connection.

The results of this experiment cannot be explained using Newtonian physics.

Conclusions We May Draw After Reading The Three Sources Above

Now it makes more sense how such phenomena as "distance healing" as well as sending or receiving thoughts may be "normal". Neither distance healing nor sending or receiving thoughts (or intentions) need to be perceived as being paranormal. This phenomenon now has a scientific basis. This helps people to understand how "distance healing" may work.

None of the above examples of how DNA can be changed should surprise us. After all, we read: "For as he thinks within himself, so is he." Proverbs 23:7 TPT. This is referring to the concept that our thoughts can change who we are.

Science is catching up to the Bible!

We are to speak to the mountain. Mark 11:23. We can interpret this as our ability to speak to something bigger than ourselves and that it would obey us.

Is changing your DNA a mountain for you? Remember, our DNA can receive and respond to frequencies. Our voice creates a frequency. And thoughts (intention) have been scientifically shown to affect the receiving DNA.

Next, we will explore the Energy Healing world. Or should we say *God's* Energy Healing world?

---

1. Genetic code. (n.d.). Genome.Gov. Retrieved May 1, 2022, from https://www.genome.gov/genetics-glossary/Genetic-Code

2. Brant A. Larsen (2019, March 9). Dr.Dispenza, Thoughts & Feelings Produce DNA Change. Brandt A. Larsen, D.C. Retrieved April 29, 2022, from https://drlarsen.com/dr

3. Grazyna Fosar and Franz Bludorf, (2002b, May). The DNA's Hypercommunication - "The Living Internet Inside Us." Bibliotecapleyades. Retrieved April 23, 2022, from https://www.bibliotecapleyades.net/ciencia/

4. Grazyna Fosar and Franz Bludorf, Scientists Prove DNA Can Be Reprogrammed by Words and Frequencies. Truth Inside Of You. Retrieved April 23, 2022, from Scientists Prove DNA Can Be Reprogrammed by Words and Frequencies (truthinsideofyou.org)

5. https://advances-journal.com/

6. https://www.faithandphysics.org/biology

6

God's Energy Healing World

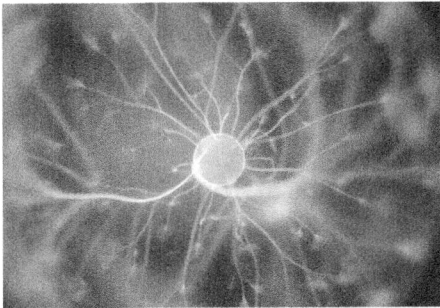

Are you curious about the picture? It comes from unsplash.com. The photographer described it as "A ball of energy with electricity beaming all over the place."

Energy causes things to move. It is inherent in an object. Any object. That is what Albert Einstein's famous equation E= MC2 tells us.

Here are Albert Einstein's own words regarding matter and energy[1]:

Concerning matter, we have been all wrong. What we have called matter is energy, whose vibration has been so lowered as to be perceptible to the senses. There is no matter.

Before Albert Einstein was born, it was Nicola Tesla who stated, "everything is energy, frequency, and vibration".

Through our discoveries in quantum physics, we can now measure what Nicola Tesla said and wrote about.

Now let us consider if the quote from Nicola Tesla regarding energy could apply to the Bible. We read: "For we have the living Word of God, which is full of energy". Hebrews 4:12 TPT. Translations other than The Passion Translation use the words "alive" and "powerful" in place of "energy". Just thought I'd bring that to your attention. Even the Word of God is energy!

But can Energy Healing be of God? Yes!

We know Einstein's equation (E=MC2) as an abstract thought. Do you think that this concept also applies to us humans as well? Science is not just an abstract idea, it describes God's work. And we are part of His work.

Remember our discussion in Chapter 3 called Who Created Energy Healing? God created the laws of science, which include quantum physics. Until now, we had a hard time explaining these invisible forces we deal with in Energy Healing.

The law of gravity is easy for us to understand because we were taught a Newtonian mindset in school. It was Newton who discovered the law of gravity. It is harder for us to grasp the concepts of quantum physics because we were trained to see through a Newtonian mindset.

A quantum physics mindset can help us grasp what is going on in Energy Healing. What is the difference between a Newtonian and a quantum physics mindset? Glad you asked! Here is your answer from academia.ed.[2]

> The Quantum world states I believe it is, and it is so.
> The Newtonian world states if I don't see it happen, it cannot be so, or rather, exist.

Quantum physics goes beyond what Newtonian physics can see.[3] Maybe we have to adjust our mindset to include quantum physics to help us see.

We can now understand how the Emotion Code Practitioner can connect with you to get accurate answers. The scientific explanation is "quantum entangled particles".

Through quantum physics, we receive the term "quantum entangled particles". The term "quantum entangled particles" describes the ability of particles to communicate with each other in an instant over unlimited distances, anywhere in the universe. This speed of communication appears to be faster than the speed of light.

Bringing that scientific explanation into the area of energy healing it explains how two people can be energetically connected. Particles from you and me can become entangled; this entanglement allows instantaneous communication.

The evidence is in! When I muscle test my client and get instant answers to yes and no questions, it is **no longer a mystery, nor is it occult. God created the laws of nature to allow for that.** There is now something of substance to answer Energy Healing critics!

The above information comes from the book titled "Frequency of the Supernatural, Revealing the Mystery of God's Quantum Universe, Empowering You to Experience The Miraculous,"[4] by Michael David.

I am so grateful there now exists a book written from a strong Christian perspective combining quantum physics, prayer, miracles, and God. This gives a better understanding of how quantum physics, created by God, can assist us in fully walking out of our mandate as a disciple of Jesus Christ and as a child of God. This book may be part of the answer you have been looking for to understand how we, as Christians, can use this wonderful gift of God we call Energy Healing.

Here are some excerpts from Michael David's book (David et al., 2018, p. back of the book). that help us grasp the enormity of God's gift to us:

The supernatural is a very real dimension.

If we could grasp the interconnection of the spirit realm and science, what difference would it make in our daily lives?

When you understand the Quantum science of the supernatural, you will be equipped with additional keys that unlock new measures of Kingdom power, intercessory authority, and supernatural miracles in your life!

This book says it more eloquently than I can.

God gave us the world of science to explain his creation. We are part of His creation.

In Energy Healing we refer to our "energy field", also as "electromagnetic field" and/or "biofield". These terms are interchangeable. What is that all about? Find out next.

1. Albert Einstein's quotes. (n.d.). https://quotefancy.com/quote. Retrieved April 21, 2022, from https://quotefancy.com/quote/763112/Albert-Einstein-Concerning-matter-we-have-been-all-wrong-What-we-have-called-matter-is

2. Joseph Vreeland, The Quantum World Versus the Newtonian World.pdf. Https://Www.Academia.Edu. Retrieved 28 April 2022, from (PDF) The Quantum World Versus the Newtonian World.pdf | Joseph Vreeland - Academia.edu

3. What Is quantum? (n.d.). Energy Wave Theory. Retrieved April 23, 2022, from https://energywavetheory.com/explanations/what-is-quantum/

4. David, M., Koevering, V. D., Brooks, S., Berguson, J., Berguson, J., Feinman, B., Feinman, T., Mainse, R., & Mainse, A. (2018). The Frequency of the Supernatural: Revealing the Mysteries of God?s Quantum Universe. Destiny Image Publishers.

7

The Human Body Energy Field

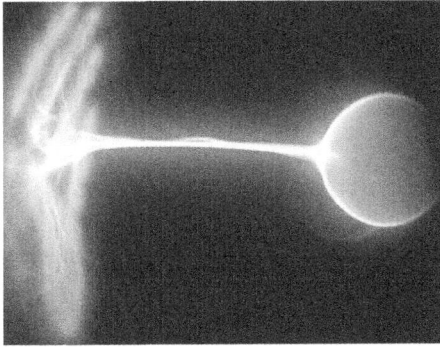

The photographer of this picture called it a "Blue static electricity arc traveling from a plasma ball to an open hand. Horizontal shot." This picture was likely shot in a type of physics interactive museum. The source of the picture is unsplash.com.

Have you ever gotten zapped by static electricity when you walked across the carpet? Why is that? Because our body has an electromagnetic field.

Why do we have an electromagnetic field? That electromagnetic field results from all the electrical processes within our cells and holding our body together. Don't just take my word for it. I have proof, or rather Jack Fraser has the proof.

Jack Fraser, who has a master's degree in physics from the University of Oxford, was quoted in an article by Forbes:[1]

> Not only is it possible that the human body creates EM (electromagnetic) fields, it is the only way you might exist as a coherent entity!

> You are an electric field — a giant electric field that holds your atoms together, and which uses other electric fields to talk to other bits of yourself.

> Everything is so cool when you break it down like this, right?

We are familiar with electromagnetic fields through their use by western medicine for diagnostic purposes. Some diagnostic tools we are familiar with are EKG (electrocardiogram), which measures the electrical activity of the heart, EEG (electroencephalogram), which measures the electrical activity of the brain and the MRI (Magnetic Resonance

Imaging), which can detect such things as aneurysms and tumors using radio waves and magnetic fields.

The electromagnetic field of the body is also called a biofield. This biofield contains information.[2]

"The biofield may be considered as the language of life." This statement comes from the PubMed document titled: "Biofield Science and Healing: History, Terminology, and Concepts".[3] Biofields are a hot topic in medical research. There are many papers on the subject within the medical community.

The term "biofield" includes what has been defined as energy medicine and was first recognized in 1992 by the Office of Alternative Medicine at the US National Institutes of Health. That same office also officially recognized the terms "distant healing" or "distant healing intention".

Let that sink in for a moment. The Office of Alternative Medicine at the US National Institutes of Health officially recognized the terms "biofield", "distant healing" and "distant healing intention" - about 20 years ago!

The US National Institutes of Health picked up from where Robert O. Becker left off.

A few years prior to when The US National Institutes of Health officially recognized the term "biofield", in 1985, the late orthopedic surgeon, Dr. Robert O. Becker, published a book called "The Body

Electric".[4] He wrote how DNA could not contain enough information in and of itself to provide us with answers to the question: what makes each person different? In the book, he also suggests there has to be "some sort of organizing field of intelligence surrounding the body."

He concluded that there must be some sort of organizing field of intelligence surrounding the body that science cannot yet detect or explain.

On the website Subtle Energies, the author elaborates further on Dr. Becker's work:[5]

> Becker's work found that there was a subtle transmission of DC voltages running throughout (our bodies) as well. These currents were found to relate to the acupuncture meridians, and he theorizes they are used as a communication network by the body to transmit information about the location and severity of an injury.

Those were interesting findings and theories that Dr. O Becker recorded. He noticed that the body runs on electricity and also theorized that currents of energy are used as a communication tool.

The Subtle Energies site goes on to say:

> Through Dr. Becker's work with frogs and salamanders to understand the regenerative, he came to the conclusion

that there must be some sort of organizing field of intelligence surrounding the body that science cannot yet completely detect or explain. Dr. Robert O. Becker contributed wonderfully to the understanding of the electrical component of our bodies.

To continue our discussion of the human body energy field, we will look at the work of Dr. Jeremy Tennant, a medical doctor. He has won many awards for his work and his contributions to the field of Ophthalmology, including cataract surgery.

In Dr. Jeremy Tennant's book called *"Healing Is Voltage, Healing Eye Diseases"*,[6] he talks about the importance of the cell being able to raise its electrical charge to enable the cell to go into a healing state. In a normal, healthy individual, the cell will naturally go into a healing state when the body needs it.

The ability to increase energy is positive for the cell. But what happens if the cell cannot increase energy? The University of Maryland Graduate School[7] gives us the answer:

A disruption in electrical currents can lead to illness.

To complete the circle of explaining electricity in the body, we confirm from the Maryland Graduate School website we have electricity throughout our body; and that it is necessary:

Electricity is required for the nervous system to send signals throughout the body and to the brain, making it possible for us to move, think, and feel.

That is straightforward.

Further to the human body energy field, you will learn in the next chapter of a recently discovered healing system designed by God our Father. Not only does this recent discovery confirm that our body is based on energy, but this energy system, called the Aleph-Tav Body System, is the deepest in the human body; and is the **source** of what we know as chakras and energy meridians.[8] Dr. Alphonzo Monzo is the author of the book called *"The Aleph-Tav Body System"*.[9] This is just a little tease of what is coming in the next few chapters.

I know everyone will question Dr. Alphonzo Monzo's faith background, so let's get that out of the way next.[10] (This information is from the bio section of his website.):

He earned a BS in Biblical Studies and Christian Ministries (Grace College and Theological Seminary, 2003). He is a graduate of the Carnegie Institute of Integrative Medicine & Massotherapy where he specialized in Myofascial—Neuromuscular Therapy, Personal Fitness Training, and Sports Massage (L.M.T. Ohio Medical Board, 2006). Dr. Alphonzo Monzo continued to earn a Master of Divinity from Christian

Leadership University (Cheektowaga, NY, 2008), a double degree from Life Training Institute as a Naturopathic Doctor (N.D.) and a Licensed Professional Naturopathic Minister (Beaumont, TX).[11]

The information in this book debunks the old argument that chakras and energy meridians are rooted in eastern religions or New Age beliefs. This argument has been used as a reason Christians should stay away from chakras and energy meridians. The knowledge in this book is pointing you to the truth. The truth is that chakras and energy meridians have their roots in the Aleph-Tav Body System within our bodies. This system was created by God to function in this way.

Let me drive the point home. It no longer matters who "discovered" the chakras and energy meridians because they originate from this deeper Aleph-Tav Body System. We shall soon discover more.

Let's now switch to how a practitioner "connects" to a person's energy field.

How a Practitioner "Connects" to a Person's Energy Field.

My clients ask me "how do you get your "yes" and "no" answers? Here is my answer:

As an Emotion Code and Body Code practitioner, I "connect" to a person's energy field to communicate with a person's subconscious mind. It is that biofield (also called electromagnetic field) that I am connecting to. That energy field contains all the information about the individual. Using the analogy of computers, we can also call that energy field a type of hard drive, since it contains all that information particular to what is unique to that individual.

I attempted to explain the foundation for the understanding of that statement earlier in the chapter.

What is the source of information? Here is your answer. **The energy field of the person themselves contains the source of the information. Our bodies function in this way. There is no need for occult knowledge.**

Back to the chapter on DNA: we learned DNA can act as receivers and transmitters. That may also be why I can access a person's biofield. My DNA and energy field can receive what their DNA is transmitting. No mystery there.

I hope the above information dispels any qualms that Energy Healing is pseudoscience or that accessing the energy of our body is necessarily occult. We have heard from two physicians, a Naturopathic Doctor, as well as the University of Maryland Graduate School, on how our bodies function on electricity.

My question to you is this...

We know God created energy and the energy system of our body. Would he also not have created a way to correct issues within that system via energy? Maybe the true name is not Energy Healing. Maybe the true name is God's Energy Healing?

What do you think?

Perhaps you are asking yourself, "Can all this really be true?" Let us examine the Bible for that answer next!

---

1. How The Human Body Creates Magnetic Fields. (2017, November 3). Https://Www.Forbes.Com. Retrieved April 30, 2022, from https://www.forbes.com/sites/quora/2017/11/03/how-the-human-body-creates-electromagnetic-fields

2. Kimberly Schipke, What is the Human Biofield? Foundation for Alternative and Integrative Medicine. Retrieved April 30, 2022, from https://www.faim.org/what-is-the-biofield

3. Rubik B, Muehsam D, Hammerschlag R, Jain S. Biofield Science and Healing: History, Terminology, and Concepts. Glob Adv Health Med. 2015 Nov;4(Suppl):8-14. doi: 10.7453/gahmj.2015.038.suppl. Epub 2015 Nov 1. PMID: 26665037; PMCID: PMC4654789.

4. R. O. Becker. (n.d.-b). The Body Electric By Robert O. Becker 1998. Https://Archive.Org. Retrieved April 23, 2022, from https://archive.org/details/thebodyelectricbyrobertobecker1998/page/n1/mode/2up

5. Life Fields and the Power of Regeneration. (n.d.). Subtle Energy. Retrieved April 23, 2022, from https://subtle.energy

6. Jeremy Tennant. (2011). Tennant Products. Https://Tennantproducts.Com. Retrieved April 23, 2022, from https://tennantproducts.com/products/healing-is-voltage-healing-eye-disease

7. How the human body uses electricity. (n.d.). Graduate U Maryland. Retrieved April 23, 2022, from https://graduate.umaryland.edu/gsa/gazette/February-2016/How-the-human-body-uses-electricity/

8. Home Page. (n.d.). Well-Being By Design. Retrieved 28 April 2022, from https://www.well-beingbydesign.com/

9. Monzo, A., 3rd, & Solomon, M. (2021). Aleph-Tav Body System. Health Restoration Technologies, LLC. Products and Affiliates. (n.d.). Retrieved 23 April 2022, from https://www.well-beingbydesign.com/the-shop

10. Practitioner Bios. (n.d.). Well-Being By Design. Retrieved May 1, 2022, from https://www.well-beingbydesign.com/practitioner-bios

11. https://www.well-beingbydesign.com/aboutus

8

How Do I Know This Is All True?

Good question! We can find the answer in the Bible. In his Word, God instructed us to judge a matter by the fruit that is borne. This is how we know if something is good for us or not. We read:

"Constantly be on your guard against phony prophets. They come disguised as lambs, appearing to be genuine, but on the inside, they are like wild, ravenous wolves! You can spot them by their actions, for the fruits of their character will be obvious. You won't find sweet grapes hanging on a thorn bush, and you'll never pick good fruit from a tumbleweed. So if the tree is good, it will produce good fruit; but if the tree is bad, it will bear only rotten fruit and deserves to be cut down and burned. You'll know them by the obvious fruit of their lives and ministries." Matthew 7:15-20 TPT.

That is a clear directive. We are to judge a matter by the fruit that is borne. What is the fruit of the Emotion Code? Here are but two of my clients who had radical transformations.

Client #1, Liz from Florida, USA:

The following is directly from Liz, herself.

As a result of our work together, my relationship with the Lord was allowed to blossom. I can hear Him speak to me and minister to me. Before our work together, I was not able to hear His voice. I was locked in self-judgement and self-hatred.

When I first came across The Emotion Code and considered the role that emotions play, I immediately dismissed it as ungodly and thought that it could not possibly be safe for Christians. It was what Dr. Caroline Leaf said that made me sit up and take notice. During an interview on a television program on TBN called "Thinking, God, and the Quantum Physics Brain", she said:

> Breakthrough neuroscientific research is confirming daily what we instinctively knew all along; what you are thinking every moment of every day becomes a physical reality in your brain and body, which affects your optimal mental and physical health.

What made the process feel safe for me was Doris prayed throughout my sessions. She will tell you herself that The Emotion Code and Body Code are only tools in the great Savior's hands. She knows that ultimate freedom comes through Christ.

Perhaps the greatest test to pass was this: "Can I forgive?". The answer is "yes". I have forgiven my abusers and have come to a place of speaking blessings over them. It is so freeing! I can now also see and feel the love of my heavenly Father.

Below, I summarize just a few things that Jesus set me free from through the help of Doris.

The false belief that I was not enough.

A loud voice in my mind telling me I was a loser.

Deep shame and anger at being sexually "touched wrong".

The lies spoken over me by a verbally abusive parent; and the lies I believed that God our Father and Jesus disliked me; they just put up with me in frustration.

Extreme fatigue: so much so that I could not take good care of my family. My children remember me as the sleeping mother.

Feelings of rejection that happened frequently, often rendering me "out of commission" for the whole day.

Many family bondages and curses.

I want to emphasize something here. From the time I first met Doris, I was totally committed to change. I worked very hard at it. I wanted to change with every fiber of my being. Our work together was the catalyst that partnered along with my commitment to seek the Lord on these matters. I believe that this partnership allowed me to see breakthroughs. That included finally being able to hear the voice of the Lord and receiving His healing balm directly.

From beginning to end, with many gaps between sessions, it was a year and a half of transformation. The healing continued even when we were not working together. What Doris began; God continued.

I write this testimony specifically for Christians; born-again Christians who believe the only way to salvation is through Jesus Christ. So many Christians are bruised and wounded. I hope they may find the same freedom as I have found.

Client #2, Krista from Wyoming, USA:

Krista was burned to over 48% of her body some twenty years prior.

She lives in Wyoming, and the winters can be cold there. Krista went from twenty years of not being able to wear socks on her feet to now being able to wear socks on her feet in the cold Wyoming winters. Prior to our word together, she no longer had sweat glands because of the deep skin burns, and after our prayer together, on the spot, she got sweat glands in her feet. How do we know she had new sweat glands in her feet? Because her feet began to sweat. For twenty years, her feet never sweat until this moment.

Her legs had also been badly burned, so much so that her legs would swell so badly down to and including her toes. Why? She said she had lost lymphatic drainage in her legs. (By no lymphatic drainage, this meant her body was no longer able to drain the fluid from her legs.) Right after our prayer, the swelling in her legs went down until her legs were the normal size. Since the burning twenty years ago, this had never happened.

Krista received both re-creative miracles because of prayer for physical healing while we were in the middle of our Emotion Code session. Immediately. Parts of her body that had been burned off (part of the lymphatic system and sweat glands) were recreated. Quite remarkable. Praise God for His goodness!

This is only part of Krista and Liz's stories. More can be found on my website.

I am grateful for these two clients willing to share their stories with you. This is but a sampling of what the Lord has done for my clients during our Emotion Code and Body Code sessions.

I share these stories not to boast, but to show you what is possible.

9

Help Others Receive God's Healing Energy.

"Everything is energy, frequency, and vibration."

Nikola Tesla.

You might remember that in the introduction, I spoke of the double standards that people can sometimes have for energy healing. They accept modern gadgets like smartphones and tablets without questioning their source or morality, yet fear other handy tools like energy healing.

Being a champion for well-being through God's healing code can be challenging when you are a Christian. There are misunderstandings regarding energy and energy healing when, in fact, energy exists as an objective reality; it is not a mystical concept. I wrote this book because I want others to know how quantum physics contains God's healing code and how we can safely access His healing code. This is a powerful discovery.

Now it's time for me to ask for your help. Just as I would not have found the guidance I needed without the help of others, there

are many people who can benefit from understanding how they can access healing energy at this very moment to help themselves function the way God created them.

By leaving a review of this book on Amazon, you can help people discover God's healing code and other safe ways he provided for us to access that energy.

Just a few sentences telling other readers how this book has helped you and what information you've found here could lead others to health and happiness. And who doesn't want to empower their own well-being?

Thank you for helping me on my quest to reveal the truth about God's healing code. God intended us to thrive. We need to knock down myths to understand that there is nothing necessarily dark or strange about energy healing. Let's make sure we help people understand the power of the wholesome tools that God has given us.

10

Finding a Safe Modality for You

T his chapter is geared towards keeping you safe in the energy healing world through finding a safe modality for you.

The following comments are from personal experience. These are potentially safe modalities:

#1 Emotion Code, and #2 Body Code

I listed the Emotion Code and Body Code[1] as potentially safe, as I have researched them and have written extensively about them in articles prior to this book. My website has additional information.

The Emotion Code and Body Code can help clients go deeply into issues by accessing the subconscious. The aspect of being able to access the subconscious (via the biofield) alone puts this tool on a different footing than any other type of modality.

Not even psychologists can access the subconscious the way the Emotion Code and Body Code can. I had the gift of being able to work with Christianne Baggen, a psychologist and therapist from The Netherlands. I am grateful for this testimony from a psychologist. This is part of her testimony found on the home page of my website:

> During and after my studies to become a psychologist and a spiritual therapist, I've done a lot of work on myself. Also, I went to retreats and educated myself further. But part of the unconscious layers of emotions that can generate blockages in the body and energetic system I haven't been able to reach fully and completely and that is what your method seems to focus on. In that sense, I'm

becoming more aware of how the work you are doing can be a valuable addition to the work of psychologists and counselors.

Another advantage of the Emotion Code and Body Code that I have seen is how the practitioner can safely access the subconscious without the client reliving or re-experiencing the event. That can be a big plus when you are dealing with highly traumatized clients of rape or other horrific events in their lives. We can spare them from reliving or re-experiencing the trauma. In this way, The Emotion Code and Body Code can be gentle and effective.

The Emotion Code & Body Code are great ways to remove painful emotions and re-balance the body energetically.

#3 Subconscious Release Technique

This is another energy healing modality that helps remove painful emotions. In that way, it is like the Emotion Code and Body Code. The subconscious Release Technique, also called SRT Global, or SRT for short, releases negative emotions related to a limiting belief program. SRT Global can remove the limiting belief along with the power of the limiting belief. SRT Global uses the breath to expel the emotion. What made me think of adding this tool to my "toolbox" was what one of the SRT Global coaches, Eileen Greer,a Subconscious Release Technique

Coach, told me, "We are releasing the lies of Satan by using the breath of God." I liked that explanation. It was scriptural.

SRT is founded by Coral Grant,[2] a Christian who gives glory to God in the mission statement of the company.

I find SRT Global very useful to remove limiting belief programs along with the painful emotions that accompany what Coral Grant calls "programs".

#4 EFT (tapping)

You can do the tapping yourself, or you can have the practitioner tap on your behalf. This is useful when you hit a painful area. Tapping is done on energy meridian points; it releases energy into the energy meridian to unblock whatever emotion is blocking it.

The one disadvantage of EFT is that it is done on conscious thoughts and memories only. In my experience, I found EFT does not reach the subconscious level; it is limited to the conscious mind.

Another disadvantage of EFT is that for it to be effective, the client needs to experience the emotion/event at the time of tapping. This is a real drawback with serious trauma such as rape, etc.

The reason I did not pursue EFT was that I found that Emotion Code and Body Code could dive deeper than other energy healing methods, as well as do so gently (by accessing the subconscious).

#5 EMDR

This is a safe and Christian-recommended modality that people can use to get rid of emotional baggage and move past trauma through specific eye movements while re-experiencing the event.

EMDR is based on biblical beliefs and practices. One shortcoming that I see is that for someone who has trauma to resolve, this method requires you to remember and relive the event to release the underlying emotions. That may be a painful experience for some people.

#6 Acupuncture (Hint: you'll be glad you read this.)

One benefit of acupuncture is that it removes blockages in the energy system. My understanding of the idea behind acupuncture is that the energy of the body flows in certain pathways, and those pathways need to be open for the body to remain healthy.

Now you will discover that acupuncture may be safer than you realize; for reasons of which you will learn next.

God created our bodies and how those bodies run. Part of the running of our bodies requires the energy to have pathways. That is what a meridian is; it is an energy pathway. God is a God of order. These energy pathways kept the flow of energy in a safe, pre-determined, designed way.

Although acupuncture (and chakras) were discovered by non-Christian cultures, neither acupuncture nor chakras require us to open ourselves up to worship other gods, nor do they, in and of themselves, open us up to spirits or the occult.

Since acupuncture and chakras were developed and practiced in eastern cultures, we associate them with being mystical and part of what many call "New Age". But is that true? We shall soon see!

The time has arrived to see the acupuncture and chakra world through a new lens. This shift in awareness may be like the big shift that occurred in the world of astronomy when one person (Hubble) changed the world view on the Milky Way and the size of the galaxy through the publication of his research.

As the shift of perception occurred in astronomy, a similar shift of perception may now happen in the world of "Energy Healing". Perhaps we can now view acupuncture, chakras, and energy meridians through a Christian lens because of the work of one person (Dr. Alphonzo Monzo).

Thanks to the work of Dr. Alphonzo Monzo III, a Biblical Naturopathic Doctor, and his book *"The Aleph-Tav Body System"*, Monzo and Solomon (2021), we learn that the energy meridians and chakras themselves, are only the results of a much deeper energy system.

I would invite you to read for yourself the details on that deeper energy system in his book called *"The Aleph-Tav Body System"*, subtitled "*Restoring the Hebrew Bio-Energetic Temple.*" Monzo and Solomon (2021)

Here is a little tidbit teaser. Dr. Monzo tells us that the Aleph-Tav Body System has command points that are related to the Hebrew alphabet, and each command point has a specific operating frequency. Interesting or what? That brings us back to the body as being energy.

Anyway, to all the naysayers that acupuncture is eastern mysticism, sorry, the truth is now revealed that *"The Aleph-Tav Body System"*, Monzo and Solomon (2021) is the root from which energy meridians and chakras arise, and, if I understand it correctly, the root from which all instructions for the organs, glands, and systems spring forth. It directs our whole body and the energy of our body. And it has God's signature throughout all of it.

So you can put away your fears of chakras, and energy meridians. The root of those is the Aleph Tav Body System, and that system has God's signature all over it, as well as His Word, literally from Aleph to Tav. The first and last Hebrew letters in the Hebrew alphabet. You don't have to trust me on that. Read the book! It is very clear.

More on this subject in section 7, next.

Aren't you glad you read this?

#7 The Aleph-Tav Body System

If you skipped to this part without reading the section above on acupuncture, you will be missing some important points. This section is a continuation of what is written in that section. (You're welcome!)

I doubt very much if you have heard of this system yet, unless you read Dr. Alphonzo Monzo's book. For those that are looking for detail, his book is for you!

Just to reiterate a bit, why do I say that chakras can be safe for Christians?

The Aleph-Tav Body System, discovered by Dr. Alphonzo Monzo, operates on a type of plasma energy, which is a type of light. Until recently, we had no instruments to measure that.

Where did you ever hear that we are light?

The Bible tells us we are made in the image of God and the Bible also tells us:

> In the beginning was the Word, and the Word was with God, and the Word was God. He was with God in the beginning. Through Him all things were made; without Him nothing was made that has been made. In him was life, and the life was the light of all mankind. John 1:1-4 NIV.

Now then, does it seem so strange that we can now find the truth of God's word contained within science?

This discovery about the plasma type of energy called the Aleph-Tav Body System changes the whole discussion relating to whether chakras and energy meridians are safe for Christians. These systems are all a creation of a loving God, and we only just discovered that!

Dr. Alphonzo Monzo III, who calls himself a Biblical Naturopathic Doctor, specializes in biophysics. We read from his website that the center he founded operates under the values and instructions set forth in the Hebrew and Apostolic scriptures.

His book talks about and shows how the Aleph Tav Body System unites the ancient Hebrew language with touch, light, oil, and sound therapies to restore wellness.

Here is a description of his book quoted from his website Shop | Well-being By Design:

> Aleph-Tav Body System: Restoring the Hebrew Bio-Energetic Temple is truly an answer to prayer for the times we are in. This book is a combination of Biblically based energy theory and hands-on applications that will also be the foundation for future courses in understanding how the "laying on of hands" can affect our health. Dr. Monzo, ND, brings the ancient and eternal instructions given by Yah center stage and demonstrates how His creative essence is written on our bodies and how He, and His Word, are the only true source of LIFE.

This is a 400-page manual that is about 1/3 theory and the rest are hands-on applications. If all you had was this book, you would be able to improve your wellness drastically. Emergency and critical needs applications are also included. Monzo and Solomon (2021)

Dr. Alphonzo Monzo's site also has music and a light system that can be used with the Aleph-Tav Body System. His book discusses the benefit of energy, frequency, and light to assist the body to heal itself. That should not surprise us as we think of the subject of Energy Healing since these tools are part of God's grand design for healing.

In Dr. Alphonzo Monzo's book on page 15, he says: "The Aleph-Tav Body System is not Kabbalah, mysticism, New Age, or occultism." I just want to make sure there is no doubt or ambiguity that this system originated from God.

Question: Do you think it is now time to rename "Energy Healing" to "*God's* Energy Healing"? He created it, after all!

#8 Other Energy Healing Methods

I am sure there are other great and safe Energy Healing methods out there. I tried to give you the best synopsis and recommendations based on the most popular ones out there, as well as what is within my knowledge range.

Next, how do you find a safe coach/practitioner?

1. Discover Healing With The Emotion Code. (n.d.). Discover Energy Healing With The Emotion Code. Retrieved April 29, 2022, from https://discoverhealing.com/

2. Mac And Coral Grant. (n.d.). If You Think You Can, You Can. SRT Global Personal Development. Retrieved April 29, 2022, from https://srtglobalpersonaldevelopment.com

11

Finding a Coach/Practitioner for You

This chapter is geared towards keeping you safe in the energy healing world through finding a safe coach/practitioner for you.

This is likely the hardest part of the entire journey. Why? There aren't many Christians doing Energy Healing work yet.

Dr. Kevin Zadai tells us we are to reclaim God's territory for his glory. Energy Healing was created by God for his children to enjoy; it is time we take it back! It belongs to us.

There are other Christian practitioners besides me, but the number remains tiny.

What makes a coach/practitioner safe?

Beyond asking God for wisdom, you might like to explore the website and even the Facebook and Instagram pages. What other modalities does the practitioner use? You can look at the articles and posts to see what interests the person has. That could tip you off to potential issues.

Look for words such as "channel", and "spirit guide". Those are tip-offs that the Christian practitioner you are looking at may not be safe for you. Tarot cards is another one. You may not be aware these things can open unwanted doors.

When you are doing energy work, you are opening yourself up. That creates permission–or legal rights–that the kingdom of darkness can use if the practitioner is or has something that is not of God. Legal rights to access you may now be available to or through the practitioners.

That is why you need to choose your practitioner with great care! That is why in the earlier chapter I mentioned "potentially" safe Energy Healing modalities. Not only do you have to consider the person doing the therapy, but you must consider the therapy itself.

And remember to cover yourself in the blood of Jesus.

Is Reiki safe? Please turn to the next chapter to find out!

12

Is Reiki Safe for Christians?

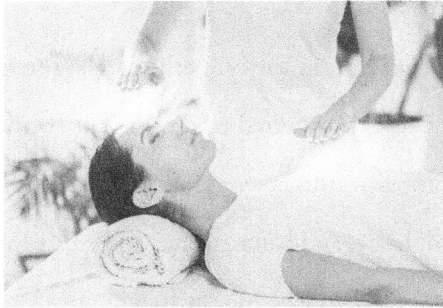

A t the risk of breaking your heart, sorry, I put this on the list of "be cautious," Reiki is passed on and practiced as more than a tool. It is also a means of transference. That is how this tool was created. The question is "Just what is being transferred?". Are you sure you know what you are *really* getting?

In the International Center for Reiki Training, over 30 different Reiki methods exist "with more being channeled all the time."

The word "channeled" should concern you right there.

The style selected for our discussion is the style of Reiki founded by Dr. Usui in 1922. This is likely the most known and popular "style".

Here are direct quotes from the International Center for Reiki Training.[1]

> Reiki was founded in Japan by a certain Buddhist monk, a Dr. Ursui who had a "spiritual awakening" after a 21-day fast.

> Reiki is not taught in the way other healing techniques are taught. It is transferred to the student by the Reiki Master during an attunement process. This process opens the crown, heart, and palm chakras and creates a special link between the student and the Reiki source.

> The Reiki attunement is a powerful spiritual experience. The attunement energies are channeled into the student through the Reiki Master. The process is guided by the Rei or God-consciousness and makes adjustments in the process depending on the needs of each student. The attunement is also attended by Reiki guides and other spiritual beings who help implement the process. Many report having mystical experiences involving personal messages, healings, visions, and past life experiences.

We also learn on that same web page:

> By receiving an attunement, you will become part of a group of people who are using Reiki to heal themselves and each other, and who are working together to heal the Earth. You will also be receiving help from Reiki guides and other spiritual beings who are also working towards these goals.

The intentions of Reiki are good and wholesome, and people often report feeling better after a Reiki treatment. All that is wonderful and desirable. However, I think people may receive more than they realize. That is why I am urging caution.

Please investigate this for yourself! I formed this opinion through my research. Please! Feel free to prove me wrong!

Up next, is hypnosis safe?

---

1. Reiki, Frequently Asked Questions. (n.d.). Https://Www.Reiki.Org/Faqs/Learning. Retrieved April 23, 2022, from https://www.reiki.org/faqs/learning

13

Is Hypnosis Safe for Christians?

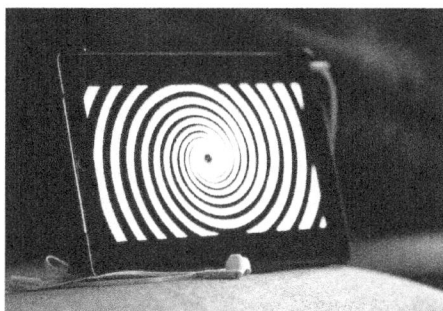

B e cautious here. Why?

Dan Duval of Bride Ministries says an absolute no to hypnosis. He has extensive experience in deliverance, so he must have his reasons.

I advise caution. Why? While you are in that hypnotic state, your conscious mind is not aware of what the hypnotist may plant in your subconscious. This puts you in a vulnerable position.

Please be cautious and feel free to prove me wrong on this one also!

14

Is Muscle Testing Safe for Christians?

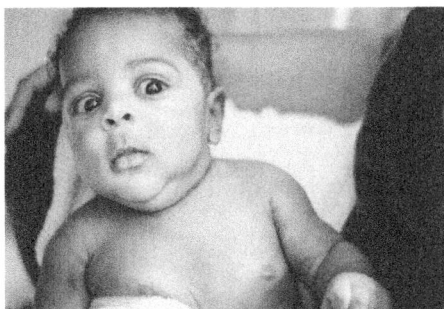

M uscle testing is a thorny issue in the Christian world. Therefore, it is with some trepidation that I introduce this subject.

Let us begin this way. Remember back in Chapter One, I asked the initial question: "Did God give you a gift that you never opened?"

Would you even consider that it is possible that muscle testing could be a gift from God? In order to answer that question, please consider these two points:

> 1. We know God made everything that exists. We read: "All things were made and came into existence through Him, and without Him was not even one thing made that has come into being."

John 1:3 AMPC. Therefore, it is reasonable to conclude that if muscle testing exists, then it owes its existence to God.

2. Satan comes to steal, kill, and destroy. We read: "The thief comes only to steal, kill, and destroy; I have come that they may have life, and have it to the full." John 10:10 NIV. Consider that it would be in Satan's character to twist our perception of something good so that, in our conclusion, we would miss this wonderful gift from God. Since Jesus told us he came for us to have life to the full, would it not seem logical that he would have provided ways to achieve that goal?

Yes, I know that there are those who misuse muscle testing, but do not let their misuse influence your perception of this potential gift from God. The enemy has thwarted *every* good gift from God. This thwarting does not change the original intent of God to provide us with something good.

Let us therefore consider reclaiming this gift so we may bring glory to God through the proper use of this gift.

Now, before we move to the muscle testing introduction, please allow me to reinforce some of what I introduced in the chapter called "God's Energy Healing World". The knowledge gained through muscle testing is possible through what scientists call "quantum entanglement". The knowledge we gain originates within the person's biofield (also known as energy field); this knowledge is not occult.

It was my hope that my saying all this would remove any remaining stumbling blocks. May you receive the beauty of truth, starting with the muscle testing introduction.

Muscle Testing Intro

Muscle testing is a technique that allows the body to communicate information from our subconscious to our conscious mind so that we can tune into what it needs. This is valuable information, given that 95% of who we are is contained within our subconscious.

We read: "You made them (humans) only a little lower than God and crowned them with glory and honor. You gave them charge of everything you made, putting all things under their authority." Psalm 8:4-5 NLT.

Pause and consider this for just a moment. How can we have charge over our subconscious mind (which God made) unless we can communicate with it? Would God not have made a way for us to communicate with the 95% of who we are?

Before we go further, please allow me to clarify the difference between muscle testing and hearing and seeing in the spirit realm. Our spirit is the part of us that sees or perceives in the spirit realm. Our spirit can discern matters beyond the body as well as what is going on inside of us. We read: "The spirit of man (that factor in human personality which proceeds immediately from God) is the lamp of the Lord, searching all his innermost parts." 1 Corinthians 2:11 AMPC.

Ideally, we would all be able to perceive clearly in the spirit realm; but that is not possible for many people. It can be helpful, therefore, to have a tool (a gift from God) that allows us a way to communicate with our subconscious mind.

God connected our subconscious mind to our body, will, and emotions. Knowledge gained through muscle testing comes from communicating with the body. If we ask, for example, what the lottery ticket number will be, we may get an answer. But who provided that answer? It could very well be something/someone not of God. That is why we need to be careful with this muscle testing, as it can be abused.

Christians are often skeptical about muscle testing. It seems mystical and is often seen as being used in energy healing. Yet, there is no reason to fear muscle testing. It is an innate and natural ability that we all have access to! Please allow me to explain further.

How Does Muscle Testing Work?

In its purest form, we do muscle testing by asking yes/no questions as we look for the truth. It is used to answer these binary questions ("yes" and "no"), and that is it.

Let's keep this simple. Just think, how do you react when someone comes towards you that you dislike? Do you wish to step back? How do you feel when someone you want to meet comes into the room?

Would you just step forward to be closer to them? Yes, you would! These unconscious reactions are your body communicating with you. Muscle testing is just another form of communication.

There are many methods of muscle testing. The common denominator in these methods is that muscles become strong or weak in response to true or false statements.

Is this too simple to be true? It **is** true! Why? We are strong when we remain within truth. We become weak when we are not within truth.

How Can I Know this Comes from God?

God is truth, and we are made in the image of God. So, it makes sense God would design us with a built-in barometer to help us recognize the truth.

"Let us make mankind in our image, in our likeness." Genesis 1:26 NIV.

"I am the way and the truth and the life." John 14:6 NIV.

God is also a God of communication.

Remember, He came to visit Adam and Eve in the garden. Why would he not make a way for us to communicate with our deepest self when he made a way for the stars to speak? He could make a way for our body to communicate with us. Why not? If the stars can speak, why not make a way for our body to communicate with us?

We read: "The heavens declare the glory of God; the skies proclaim the work of His hands. Day after day they pour forth speech." Psalm 19:1-4 NLT.

Sounds poetic, but scientists have discovered that even stars produce sound! Perhaps the bible is correct by saying that the stars "pour out speech." There is a YouTube entitled "Singing Stars" by Nature Video that allows us to "hear" these singing stars, in case that topic interests you.

If muscle testing is an accurate form of communication, as stated previously, God must have created it. We read: "He made all things visible and invisible." Colossians 1:16 TPT.

Is Muscle Testing the Same as Applied Kinesiology?

Can I Still Trust it if I Don't Believe in Applied Kinesiology?

Muscle testing is NOT Applied Kinesiology.

I would like to help you sort out this point of confusion.

Applied Kinesiology is a system of diagnosis where certain muscles are correlated to certain organs.

The Emotion Code and other energy healing modalities are also using muscle testing as a tool, but in service of a different end goal. We are not looking for weak muscles to point us to their corresponding organs.

We have a built-in function that can discern truth from a lie. It is this modality that allows us to muscle test.

As a result, it is possible to reject the Applied Kinesiology system of diagnosis without disbelieving muscle testing. If we were to continue to hold on to doubts about Applied Kinesiology, it would be like "throwing out the baby with the bath water".

Muscle testing can be done in two ways; either on someone else's behalf or in person. When done from a distance, muscle testing answers are transmitted to the other party using thought and quantum entanglement. Allow me to show you more about transmission through thought.

Answers From Science

Here are 3 examples from science proving that communication can occur via thought alone:

- The paper published in August 2014 called, "Conscious Brain-to-Brain Communications in Humans Using Non-Invasive Technologies". This study shows the conscious transmission of information between human brains.[1]

- In an article titled, "Wheelchair Makes the Most of Brain Control" we read how a wheelchair system can give paralyzed people more mobility using only the thoughts coming from their brain.[2]

-

DARPA - the USA Department of National Defense research arm - is "paying scientists to invent ways to read instantly, soldier's minds... to create thought control weapons." Live Science published this article on May 23, 2019. Creating thought weapons shows the government is serious about the science behind the idea of communicating via thoughts.[3]

Dr. Caroline Leaf, a Christian Cognitive Neuroscientist, speaks in her TEDx talk[4] about the power of thought to change our brains, and that thought travels vast distances almost instantaneously. She says:

Every thought influences every single cell of your body at quantum speed, which is much faster than the speed of light. Your thinking changes the physical. Mind is over matter. Mind influences matter.

What should we conclude? God established science, and he also established the gift inside of us that acts like a natural lie detector, even at a distance.

Biblical Perspective on the Power of Thought

In the beginning, God spoke. And it was. Genesis 1:3.

He was not holding play dough in his hand while forming the earth. No, He spoke, and vast distances became populated with matter and form, including our earth and everything in it. His thoughts and verbal commands traveled across space and affected matter.

God purposed within to make all things; then he spoke. God has given us this same ability as He made us in His image.

How powerful are our thoughts and intent? Thoughts have power. We are told our imagination carries the same power as action. Matthew 5:27-28.

To drive home the point here about the relationship between thought, words, and intent, consider this. In Genesis 1:3 where it says: "God spoke", that word for "spoke" in the original Hebrew language is "amar"[5] which means to "say, speak, (voice) answer, think (thought) or intend."

In the original language of the Bible, there is no difference between speaking, thinking, and intention. This proves the power of thought.

Distance Healing in the Bible

Here are three instances of distance healing found in the bible.

The first one is recorded in Mark 7:24. In this story, we are told of how a gentile woman's daughter was possessed by an evil spirit. The mother begged Jesus to release her child from the control of the demon. What was the answer she received? Jesus said, "Because you have answered so well, I have healed your daughter." When the mother returned, she found her daughter free from the demon.

We heard of the second instance of distance healing regarding the centurion and his servant in an earlier chapter.

The third instance has to do with the son of a nobleman as recorded in John:46-54 TPT. The story takes place in Cana of Galilee, where Jesus made the water into wine. A certain nobleman's son was sick. He begged Jesus to come right away, as his son was at the point of death. Jesus replied to him: "Unless you people see signs and wonders, you will by no means believe." Then Jesus told him to go his way, that his son "lives". The man believed, and it was so.

There are likely many other distance healing stories that could have been written in the bible, however we are told: "Jesus did many other things as well. If every one of them were written down, I suppose that even the whole world would not have room for the books that would be written." John 21-25 NIV.

Maybe you never noticed it before, but distance healing **is** in the bible. So the next time someone asks you where distance healing is in the bible, you have an answer for them.

In Summary

We have seen that there are scientific experiments and three bible stories showing that thoughts can travel vast distances. And we have heard from Dr. Caroline Leaf, who has spent her career proving how thoughts affect matter. From what we have learned, we can confirm the bible shows the power of thought.

Would you like a bit of help to learn how to muscle test? This information is waiting for you in the bonus chapter!

---

1. Grau, Carles & Ginhoux, R. & Riera, Alejandro & Nguyen, Thanh & Chauvat, Hubert & Berg, Michel & Amengual Roig, Julià L & Pascual-Leone, Alvaro & Ruffini, Giulio. (2014). Conscious Brain-to-Brain Communication in Humans Using Non-Invasive Technologies. PloS one. 9. e105225. 10.1371/journal.pone.0105225.

2. Graham-Rowe, D. (2020, April 2). Wheelchair Makes the Most of Brain Control. MIT Technology Review. https://www.technologyreview.com/2010/09/13/200477/wheel chair-makes-the-most-of-brain-control/

3. Gent, E. (2019, May 23). The Government Is Serious About Creating Mind-Controlled Weapons. livescience.com. https://www.livescience.com/65546-darpa-mind-controlled-weap ons.html

4. Science of Thought. (2015, March 16). [Video].

5. https://hebrew4christians.com/Glossary/Word_of_the_Week/Ar chived/Emor/emor.html

15

Summary

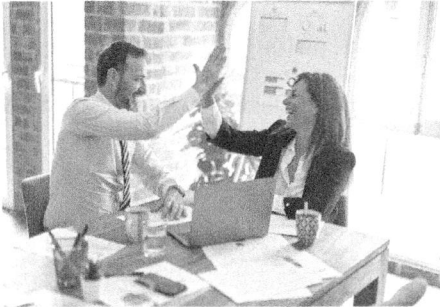

I hope you enjoyed discovering such things as biofields; learning that DNA can respond to voice, discovering the true origin of the energy meridians and, how the Aleph-Tav Body System is the root of chakras, and how God's presence is within it all.

We read earlier how the Hubble telescope showed that the Milky Way was not the entire universe, but a speck in the universe. We can now allow these recent scientific discoveries in quantum physics to give us an understanding of God's provision of Energy Healing; as his gift to us. Let us open our eyes to the gifts of God that await our discovery. The gift of energy healing is God's gift to us.

Yes, we can also use our Christian authority to speak miracles into being.

Suffering no longer needs to hold us captive. Jesus came to set the captives free.

Jesus paid the price. He said: "I have come to give you everything in abundance, more than you expect–life in its fullness until you overflow!" John 10:10 TPT.

Do you want the abundant life He promised? He made the way!

Enjoy the bonus chapter on how to easily learn to muscle test. Coming next!

16

Bonus Chapter: Easily Learn How to Muscle Test

D id you know that learning muscle testing is like riding your first grown-up bike with training wheels? That seems awkward at first, so it is with learning how to listen to your body's signals. At first you may have a hard time tapping into your "knower", but with consistent use of your muscle testing skill, you will learn how to tune in to your "knower". The training wheels on the grown-up bike are like muscle testing. At some point, you won't need those training wheels anymore.

I can speak from experience. Some time after my clients learn how to muscle test, they begin to "hear" and "see" what God wants them to see and hear. They no longer have to rely on someone else for that. This gift of muscle testing is so valuable!

Imagine how you will cherish being able to muscle test! You can now decide more easily what to put in your body. For example, imagine running to the grocery store and struggling to choose the best quality olive oil for you! If you could muscle test, you would know which one. This could save you money as well.

Muscle testing is a learned skill. Everyone mastering a new skill must work at getting the feel. Perfecting your new muscle testing skill just takes some time.

Easy Tips To Help You Learn How To Muscle Test

In the beginning, as you try to get the feel of muscle testing, consider implementing this learning into your everyday life. Waiting for the water to boil for your tea? Spend that time practicing your muscle testing. Waiting on hold while on the phone? Use that time to practice your muscle testing. You get the idea!

Before you decide what to test, make it easy on yourself! Pick something that is "yes" or "no". Say, for instance, you are wearing a blue pullover. You could say, "I am wearing a blue pullover." You know the answer is a "yes". This gives you the awareness of what it's like. Next, you could state, "I am wearing a red pullover." The answer is a "no". This makes you aware of what a "no" feels like.

To become proficient, employ this type of simple, clear questioning regularly. Repeat this many, many times daily at the beginning, if you can. Remember that it takes time to build new connections in the brain. You should expect that it may require several weeks of practice before you become confident. That is ok!

Now, let's look at one of the easiest "muscle testing" techniques to learn. It is called the sway test. If you haven't seen it, let me explain.

The Sway Test

Think of it this way. Have you ever picked up someone from the airport? Perhaps someone you care about? What was your first unconscious reaction when you saw that person? Did you move forward towards them? I bet you did! You wanted to be with that person, so you moved forward towards them! THAT is a yes.

A "yes" is that simple to remember.

Which direction is a "no"? Perhaps this will help you remember. Suppose you are at the airport, and you see someone you don't like. Don't you instinctively move away? Moving backwards is a "no".

If you have seen pictures or videos of the sway test, you see them move forward or backwards. The examples I gave above are to help you easily remember which way is "yes" and which way is "no".

There are different ways of using your hands to muscle test. You can learn more than one way of muscle testing as an alternative way to check yourself.

How Does Muscle Testing Work?

God made us in His image; He is truth. We are strong when we remain in truth. We naturally become weak when we are NOT in truth. This explains how muscle testing works.

Muscle testing is an integral part of the Emotion Code and Body Code. It is how we can find the trapped emotions or imbalances in the body that need our help. Since one of the primary tools I use is the Emotion Code, I will include a brief explanation of how to apply muscle testing to the Emotion Code chart. Perhaps this can help you learn this skill for yourself.

Using The Emotion Code Chart

At first, it might seem scary to see all those emotions listed. You might wonder how to find the right emotion.

With a little practice, you see it becomes easier and easier.

Look at the chart and speak your questions out loud. Next, ask: "Is the emotion in column A or B?" Once you get that answer, ask this. "Is the emotion in the even or odd row?" Once you find the row, check each emotion. The emotion making your body weak will indicate the trapped emotion you are looking to release!

You won't need to continue to say the question out loud as time goes on. Just by looking at the word, your body will respond. It takes a little practice, but it becomes easier and easier.

Occasionally, you will check each of the emotions in the row and realize that it is none of them. In that case, ask: "Is this emotion inherited?" It likely is. Go through the list again to see which one it is.

Here, you need to find whether the trapped emotion is inherited through the mom or dad. Then ask how many generations back. Then ask if you can release the emotion now. If the answer is a yes, then that should take care of it. If the answer is a no, just ask if you need to find something more. It could be another trapped emotion.

Word of Caution

Once you get comfortable with muscle testing, you might think to ask a question of the future. That is not a good idea.

Our subconscious mind knows a lot more than we realize, but it does not know the future. If you try to ask about the future, you are no longer tapping into your subconscious mind. THAT is when you are likely consulting something not of God. Just wanted to give you a "heads up" on that.

Influencing a person's behavior (without their consent and knowledge) could certainly fall into the witchcraft realm. We don't want to do that. For this reason, we should **not** do energy work on someone without their permission. We want to use our muscle testing in a godly manner.

In Closing

Muscle testing is a gift of God, given to help us communicate with our bodies, and with people's permission, we can help them in this way, as well.

17

Can You Help Others Harness God's Healing Energy?

We are all energy... and by now, I'm sure you know God is the ultimate source of this energy we need for our well-being. Will you help me spread the news about His intention for us to receive His gift?

All you have to do is leave your honest opinion of this book on Amazon, and other people like you will find the guidance they need to embrace godly energy healing techniques.

LEAVE A REVIEW!

Let's help as many people as we can free trapped emotions and other blocked energy to enable them to receive this well-being. Thank you so much for helping me out.

>>> Click here to leave your review on Amazon.

(If you are reading this in print form, all you need to do is go back to Amazon, click on the book. You will find the place to leave a review is located at the lower part of the page. Or, if you prefer, you can go back to your orders page in Amazon for when you purchased the book, and on the right side of that section, you will see a button you can click to leave a review.)

Thank you!

Epilogue

C ongratulations!
   My goal was to serve you and make a positive difference in your life by inspiring you with the truth.

I am proud of you for making the significant decision to better yourself by reading this book. You want to improve your life and I admire you for that.

My hope is for you to receive all that God has for you.

Whether you achieve the goal of your wellness through Energy Healing is solely up to you. No one can promise or guarantee what level of success you will achieve.

However, by knowing the truth, you are now empowered to better receive the gifts God has provided for you.

YOU CAN DO IT - THE TIME TO START IS NOW!

Again, congratulations!

O Lord, what an amazing variety of all you have created! Wild and wonderful is this world you have made, while wisdom was there at your side. Psalm 104:24 TPT.

Acknowledgments

Through the years, many have shared ideas, mentoring, and support that have impacted my life each in a different way. It is impossible to thank everyone and I apologize for anyone not listed. Please know that I appreciate you greatly.

One of the most important people I wish to thank is Dr. Bradley Nelson, who wrote the book "The Emotion Code". That was the book that started me on this journey. Had Dr. Bradley Nelson not written that book, none of this would have come about. Thank you, Dr. Bradley Nelson, from all of us. We love you!

I thank God for all the blessings I am fortunate to have in my life! Special gratitude must go to Mom and Dad, Archile Morissette, Denise, Gord, Stephanie and Eric, Vickie and Maurice Dolenuk, Marie and Gord Kanne, Pritpal Jhass, Noelle Turpinat-Johnston, Janine Bailey, David Hooper, Nicole Taylor, Amanda Maddox, Tinsley Maddox, Mickey Wilson, Robyn Van Linge, Shalla O'Keefe, Alicia

Pirozzolo, Tammy Taylor, Amanda Lee, Kimberly and Donald Palendat, Selorm Agbevieko, Rev. Mike Nwosu, Michael Lane, Eileen Greer, Schlyce Jimenez, Dan Duval, Alphonzo Monzo III, Nicole Williamson, Alicia Bozza, Sherri Favors, Kurtis Bouskill, Jackie Gale, Coral Grant, Manoj Varghese, Alfred E. Hammer, David McMillan, Amanda Buys, Kimberly Kubitza, Gerbrand Samuel de Beer, Karen Friesen, Shelbie Rezendiz, Renita and Scott Brannan, Marie Bileski, Wendy Daldren, Esther Elias, Phil Tarnapolski, Pritpal Jhass, Grudeep Jhass, Rev. M. Nwosu, Marilyn Bedard, Terry Bell, Dr. Anthony Lockwood, Dr. Robert Henderson, Katie Souza, Dr. Kevin Zadai, Dr. Francis Myles, John Ramirez, Dr. Dennis Carrington, Wendy Stephens, Grace Pryzner, and Ani Berberian, Marie Bileski, Willard and Betty Thiesen, Pat and Wendy Smolinski as well as Clinton and Tyler.

Also By The Author

Would you like to unlock the godly inheritances you just discovered? The

next book will help you do just that! Coming soon.

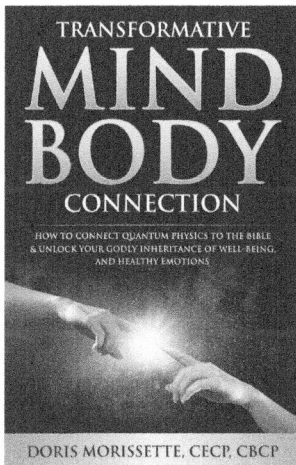

About The Author

I am so pleased to meet you!

Retired after 23 years as a Registered Nurse, I continued to "alleviate suffering" even after I hung up my uniform for the last time.

I am dedicated to help you discover and unlock a mostly unknown godly inheritance; and equip you to fulfill your destiny.

I have been a Certified Emotion Code and Body Code Practitioner since 2017. Energy healing seemed like a natural fit. While working on my theology degree through the Warrior Notes School of Ministry and as a student at Bride Ministries Institute (Dan Duval), I also became an author.

I have also taken special trainings through Robert Henderson ministries (The Court Room of Heaven) and Dr. Francis Myles and Katie Souza, (Idols Riot Intensive Healing School, I Speak To The Earth, and Sons of the Light).

People that come for the Emotion Code and Body Code often also need advanced inner healing ministry (which can include healing the inner child), ministry to the human spirit, and deliverance. The Bride Intensives in these three areas have been a great asset.

In case you are not familiar with Bride Ministries,[1] here is an excerpt for you:

> BRIDE Ministries International is a Christian church and family of believers; centered on the gospel of the Kingdom of God. God's kingdom is revealed when the afflicted are delivered; when the sick are healed; when miracles manifest, and when the name of Jesus Christ is exalted. We specialize in unlocking these realities in a practical way through equipping men and women with tools for advanced spiritual warfare, deliverance, inner healing, and discipleship to maturity in Christ.

While helping people to restore their lives; I have seen transformations that seemed miraculous. This book could not contain all those stories.

My website: www.RestoredForLifeNow.com

YouTube Channel: Restored For Life NOW

May God richly bless you!

---

1. Bride Ministries International—Strategic Equipping
   (bridemovement.com)

Made in United States
Orlando, FL
17 February 2025

58625686R00066